BRANDED

Branded™

Some WrapperRhymes

Helena Nelson

RED SQUIRREL PRESS

First published in 2019 by Red Squirrel Press
36 Elphinstone Crescent
Biggar
South Lanarkshire
ML12 6GU
www.redsquirrelpress.com

Typesetting and design by Gerry Cambridge
e: gerry.cambridge@btinternet.com

A CIP catalogue record is available from the British Library.

ISBN: 978 1 910437 82 7

This pamphlet is printed in Scotland by Love and Humphries.
ww.lhnow.co.uk

Contents

Foreword

Ted Hughes liked to eat Tunnock's Caramel Wafers and developed a habit of scribbling rhymes onto the wrappers. Or so the story goes. At least three of these scraps of lesser literature have been preserved, signed in the bard's own hand. In 2011, one of them was on loan to the St Andrews University Museum, where it was tastefully displayed in a glass box. Someone from the Scottish Poetry Library captured this in a photograph and posted it on Twitter. The Ted Hughes poem went, in the great and glorious tradition of Ogden Nash, like this:

> To have swallowed a Crocodile
> Would make anybody smile
>
> But to swallow a Caramel Wafer
> Is safer.

Designer and poet Nick Asbury (@asburyandasbury) was around on Twitter that day. So was the Glasgow design studio @effektive, and @inpressbooks. A sparky exchange took place about WrapperRhymes as a genre that could be fun to promote.

And so it was that Nick Asbury and Effektive Studio developed a Tumblr site dedicated to poetic outpourings on candy wrappers. The first example was penned by Nick Asbury on Chewit papers (31 May, 2011). Tumblr proved a superb visual medium for displaying the original, written-on packaging.

Then open submissions were invited. Punters were to compose rhymes according to a few simple rules:

1. The words were to be written directly onto wrappers and capped at 50.
2. Confectionery and snack products were preferred but the packaging of any edible product was acceptable.
3. Some relationship between food product and rhyme was expected.

And what a range of goods and goodies emerged! They included Jelly Babies, Yorkies, Mars Bars, Toblerones, Yorkshire Tea, Walkers Crisps, Fisherman's Friends, Kitkats, Milky Bar Buttons, a whole box of Black Magic, and so on. The site was a source of delight and entertainment, with new additions periodically publicised on Twitter. The whole experiment ended, as it had begun, with a magnificent piece from Nick Asbury on a Viscount biscuit paper (31 May, 2012).

But there's a more embarrassing element to this backstory. All editors know about the kind of poets who turn into pests, poets who bombard them with innumerable poems.

During the year of WrapperRhymes I turned into one of those pests. I bought special pens for writing on any surface. I bought every form of candy you can imagine, and then moved on to flour, sugar and soup. I'm ashamed to say I posted Nick Asbury one of my WrapperRhymes almost every week for at least six months. What could he possibly do with them all? In the end, the craze wore off, though I find myself subject to periodic relapse.

This poetic form has changed my attitude to food wrapping. I relish snacks in proportion to the writing potential of their wrappers. Paper is best. WrapperRhymes are therefore eco-friendly.

I hope *Branded* will amuse, as well as encourage others to try their hand. If Ted Hughes can do it, so can we. WrapperRhymes are a proven remedy for writer's block, as well as a respectable reason for buying any candy product. Inspiration is almost always to be found in the small-print list of ingredients (see page 34). It may be wise, however, to invest in an indelible marker—the kind of pen that will write on anything.

The WrapperRhyme Tumblr site is, alas, no longer in existence. Like the writers of *Fawlty Towers* (and unlike the author of *Branded*) the editor knew when to stop.

H.N.

Barratt Candyland Candy Sticks

A banker reflects

More often than not
I have lost the plot
and the world of finance mocks.

I need the fix
of some candy sticks
in a little cardboard box.

Fox's Classic

Though there were none in the Jurassic,
nevertheless, this Fox's Classic
(of biscuits, the epitome)
has ruled since 1853.
I'll say it once. I'll say it twice.
This biscuit is extremely nice.

Nestlé's Drifter Bar

My message may escape you—
I'm a subtle meaning-shifter—
but since you failed to get my drift,
you also missed my Drifter.

Thirteen Ways to Eat a Malteser

1. Fresh from the freezer
2. Deep fried in batter
3. Grilled on ciabatta
4. Grated on custard
5. Rolled up in mustard
6. Stabbed with a fork
7. Thin-sliced with pork
8. Toasted with cheese
9. Curried with peas
10. Stir-fried with rocket
11. Liquidised (lick it)
12. Light-boiled (just crack it)
13. Straight from the packet

Mars Revels[1]

You do look, my love, emptied of all thought
As if you were dismayed: be cheerful, dear,
Though Revels now are ended. The packet,
As I foretold you, was delicious and
Is melted into air, into thin air
As doth befit a 35-gram bag.
Say no to multi-pack. We are such stuff
As cremes are made of and our little tums
Are rounded with a sweet.

Noir

Lindt Excellence Orange Intense Chocolate Bar

Grateful as a child was I
for porridge in my porringer

but now for breakfast I rely
on chocolate that is orange-er

and—even when I'm pretty skint—
I like to have it made by Lindt.

Fry's Turkish Delight

Back in 1866 (a true story)

The weather was dark.
The weather was murky.
Fry and his mother
booked two weeks in Turkey.

They loved it by day.
They loved it by night.
The Frys were surprised
by their Turkish Delight.

Moral:
Once bitten
twice Fry.

Cadbury's Flake

At ten o'clock—
at coffee break—

I ate a slice
of carrot cake

and then a bar
of coconut bake

and then a marshmallow-
and-chocolate shake

topped with
a crumbly, flaky flake.

It was a mistake
to add the flake

and when I think of it
I quake.

Flake Allure[2]

I have not purchased heretofore
the chocolate bar named Flake Allure.

What mini marketing kerfuffle
has flake 'enrobed' in velvet truffle?

And is this flaky truffle nice—
or just a way to raise the price?

I've sampled one. It did restore
some slight *esprit* to a doubtful *corps*.

The 'maxi-pack' contains five more.
I've eaten three. No, no—it's four—

the wrapper-count tells true. But truer:
how I wish I'd eaten fewer.

Toffee Crisp

A Toffee Crisp is crisper
than that chocolate bar called Wispa.

Cadbury's Wispa

A: I see this Wispa 'may contain nuts'.
    But how did they get *in*?
B: They are hiding in the factory, Sir
    and desperately thin.

Knorr Chicken Stock Cube

This chicken stock cube wrapper's very small—
it's neither Knorr. I find when writing on it
my best's reduced to what will fit withal
and so this is a quatrain, not a sonnet.

Hellmann's Real Mayonnaise

'Brings out the best'

How shall I use thee? Let me count the ways
in which I make the best of things with Hellmann's Mayonnaise.

Cadbury's Fudge

After consuming just one finger
Thoughts of another sometimes linger.
Stuff the advert. It's just a bluff.
A finger of fudge is *not* enough.[3]

Jelly Baby Blues

O jelly babies[4] in a box for just two quid, my premise is
that our encounter will be brief and I, alas, your Nemesis!

I note your names begin with B—Brilliant, Big Heart, Bubbles,
Baby Bonny, Boofuls, Bumper. Salivation doubles.

Real fruit juice. Yes, indeed, my dears. And everybody savours
the way your colours are natural, and so are all your flavours.

How touching your wee faces are! Your smiles are winning assets,
a credit to the Cadbury's sweet once solely owned by Bassetts.

I have no fear of Spanish flu, malaria or rabies
but I fear the fate that now awaits my darling jelly babies.

Ode to a Kitkat

One hundred and seven calories!
  Oh how I love to linger
On even fifty-three and a half
  Of your individual finger.

Oh KitKat, KitKat—this I know:
  You will not make me fat
Unless I eat sixteen of you
  And I probably won't do that.

Allinson's Extra Strong White Bread Flour

Its rise to power
  Will not take long.
This flour won't cower.
  This flour is strong.

This flour is white.
  This flour can grow.
This flour is right
  For proving dough.

It makes a loaf
  So white and pure
That every oaf
  Wants several more.

Those investing
  Have even said:
*This is the best thing
  Since sliced bread!*

Just Add Water ... (Wright's Bread Mix)

Sunflower, sesame, poppy and kibbles,
nine types of grain—a noblesse of nibbles!
What a delight! Wright's Mixed Grain
wrightfully wrises again and again.
If you want to make dough,
it's the wright way to grow
(though prove it too long
and Wrights can go wrong).

Wanted

He had a Bounty
on his head.
That's why they shot him
(so they said).

Green&Blacks Organic 35g Bar

This charming little block of choc
will never make you run amok.

In fact, organic cocoa butter
makes most mayhem into mutter,

meaning Green&Black's Organic
brings beatitude, not panic

and (in time) the two-tone wrapper
acts as a subtle poem-trapper.

Jameson's Ruffle Bar: Raspberry

My Raspberry Ruffle has been snaffled.
Where did it go? Alas, I'm baffled.

I'm stuffed, I'm stupefied, I'm stifled.
My Raspberry Ruffle has been rifled.

Twix Fino[5]

Remember that old Twix?
Two chocolatey sticks

with toffee and biscuit
for those who would risk it.

Now there's Twix Fino
which keeps you more leano.

Eat one for dinner.
You'll shortly be thinner

and you're never on your own-io
once you're skin and bonio.

Cadbury's Curly Wurly

First Witch: When shall we three meet again?
                  In thunder, lightning or in rain?

Second Witch: When the curly-wurly's done,
                  When the couverture has run,
                  When the wrapper's lost and won.

Third Witch: That will be ere set of sun.
                  But wait—the Curly Wurly's *gone!*
                  I don't get it. Who ate it?

Hotel Chocolat: Caramel Tiddly Pot

This dainty little tiddly pot
  of dinky caramel chocolate drops
is—some would say—a fiddly pot
  but I say it's the tops.

To get some more (a less piddly pot)
  I'd ransack several shops.
Its only disadvantage is
  it does not hold a lops.*

*I meant of course
'a lot'. Perhaps
the wrapper caused
a lapse.

Baxter's Crinkled Beetroot in Sweet Vinegar

O Baxter's beetroot ruby-red
I have eaten you in bed
and in the bath. Yes, yes, it's true.
I've had you in the kitchen too
for breakfast, lunch and afternoon tea.
I love you so. My heart is sprinkled
with slice upon slice of Baxter's crinkled.
O beetroot, if you'll be true to me,
then I'll beetroot to you.

Co-op Ready To Cook Italian Tomato Chicken

Before

O Co-op Italian Tomato Chicken
you say you are 'ready to cook'.
How ready is 'ready'? I'm feeling unsteady
now that (instead of my book)
I've read through the list of ingredients
inscribed very small on your label—
all 37. Can this make good sense?
We may not have room on the table.

After

This 'ready meal' has been consumed.
Dear Co-op—for goodness sake—
the first 36 were—well, *okay*—
but the kale was a mistake.

Alliance[6]

Walkers Ready Salted Crisps
are to the potato

what paella is to Spain
and Stoltenberg to NATO.

Alltricks Powerbar Energize

This Power Bar
will power far
better a cyclist
than you are.

Heinz Tomato Ketchup (57 Varieties)

Oh look what happened
  to this brown toad
who simply attempted
  to cross the road!
If he could, he would
  express remorse
for ending his days
  as plain brown sauce.

So look right, look left,
  and then right again.
This careful stuff is
  a terrible pain
but at least there's a chance
  you will not fetch up
looking like Heinz
  Tomato Ketchup.

¹ Mars Revels arrived on the scene in 1967, and the original fillings were orange crème, coconut, toffee, peanut, Galaxy counters, Maltesers and (allegedly) Turkish Delight. I am allergic to peanuts, and used to play Revel Roulette. Eating them is now less risky. Current centres are: orange, coffee, raisin, Maltesers, chocolate and toffee. Coffee was evicted (see Revels eviction advert of 2008) at one point in favour of strawberry but then brought back as a counter-intuitive selling point.

² Flake Allure was one of a number of limited edition Flakes, which have also included Orange Flake, Flake Mint and Flake Snow ('Snowflake' until 2003). The last of these was a white chocolate bar dipped in milk chocolate. (Ugh!) Flake had a jingle that those alive at the time will almost certainly remember: 'Only the crumbliest, flakiest chocolate, tastes like chocolate never tasted before'.

³ Cadbury's fudge finger was launched as long ago as 1948 under the name Milk Fudge, which later became just Fudge. In the 1970s through to the early 1990s Fudge was advertised with the slogan 'A finger of fudge is just enough to give your kids a treat'. This memorable jingle was devised by Mike d'Abo, former lead vocalist of Manfred Mann (recruited in 1966 when Paul Jones went solo). The tune really belongs to the traditional English folk song 'The Lincolnshire Poacher'. D'Abo poached it.

⁴ The Wikipedia page on Jelly Babies is an education. Some version of these candies can be traced back as far as 1885. Various jellied creatures have been produced by different manufacturers over the years but my Blues were written on a yellow box of Bassett's and celebrates (if that's the right word) the 2011 incarnation of the babes, each colour of which now had its own slightly gruesome name. So the green one

(lime flavour) is Boofuls, while the black one (blackcurrant) is Bigheart. You don't need to know this. But you may like to know about the popular classroom science experiment known as 'screaming jelly babies', in which you put a baby or two into an oxidising agent and stand well back....

[5] Twix Fino was launched in 2010, one of many variations on the original Twix. There have been some curious versions of this sweetmeat. For example, Mint Slice billu (2005–6, Australia) was a chocolate butter cookie, chocolate mint caramel and dark chocolate. It is not just imagination that the bar has got smaller over the years. Between 2012 and 2013 the standard UK Twix shrank from 58g to 50g. This is quite slimming in itself.

[6] Jens Stoltenberg (b. 16 March 1959) is a Norwegian politician. At the time of writing, he serves as the 13th Secretary General of the North Atlantic Treaty Organisation (NATO).WrapperRhymes are often remarkably modernist in their references.

A NOTE ON THE TYPE

This pamphlet is set in Frutiger Serif, Adrian Frutiger
and Akira Koyabashi's re-envisioning of Frutiger's
Meridien (1957). It is a very versatile text face
that in its full version comes in twenty weights,
including light, condensed and heavy.